Astro-Man

Paul Cheshire

SERIES CONSULTANT: LORRAINE PETERSEN

NASEN House, 4/5 Amber Business Village, Amber Close, Amington, Tamworth, Staffordshire B77 4RP

Rising Stars UK Ltd.
22 Grafton Street, London W1S 4EX
www.risingstars-uk.com

Text © Rising Stars UK Ltd.

The right of Paul Cheshire to be identified as the author of this work has been asserted by him in accordance with the Copyright, Design and Patents Act 1998.

Published 2009

Cover design: Burville-Riley Partnership
Illustrator: Neil Smith
Text design and typesetting: Andy Wilson, for Green Desert Ltd
Publisher: Gill Budgell
Editor: Catherine Gilhooly
Series consultant: Lorraine Petersen

All rights reserved. No part of this publication may be reproduced, stored in a retrieval system, or transmitted in any form by any means, electronic, mechanical, photocopying, recording or otherwise without the prior permission of Rising Stars UK Ltd.

British Library Cataloguing in Publication Data.
A CIP record for this book is available from the British Library

ISBN   978-1-84680-501-1

Printed by Craft Print International Limited, Singapore

CONTENTS

Characters		4
Scene 1:	TROUBLE IN THE TOILET	7
Scene 2:	DOCTOR M	19
Scene 3:	AN EVIL PLAN	29
Scene 4:	ANDY THINKS FAST	37
In the chatroom...		46

Characters

Paul
A DJ who loves hip hop.

Andy
Paul's best friend. He loves comics.

Dan
Paul's older brother and a bit of a bully.

Characters

Doctor M
Comic book baddie.

Astro-Man
Comic book hero.

Narrator
The narrator tells the story.

Scene 1

TROUBLE IN THE TOILET

Narrator It is Sunday. Paul and Andy are in Paul's room. Paul is on his decks and Andy is drawing a new comic. Suddenly the lights start flashing on and off and Paul's decks stop working.

Andy Is it meant to sound like that?

Paul That's not me.

Andy Weird!

Astro-Man

Narrator	The lights continue to flash.

Paul Let's check it out.

Andy O-Okay.

Narrator	Andy and Paul walk round the house. A distant sound makes Andy jump.

Andy Urgh! What's that?

Narrator	Paul jumps.

Paul Don't freak me out like that!

Narrator	Paul's older brother Dan is snoring in the next room.

Paul You idiot, that's Dan.

Andy Well, you jumped.

Scene 1   Trouble in the toilet

Paul   Only because you made me jump!

Narrator   The lights are still flashing on and off
but Dan is *still* asleep on the sofa.

Paul   Look at him. He's so lazy.

Dan   (*Snores*)

Andy   Let's wake him up.
Something's not right about this.

Paul   Oh will you stop with that?

Andy   Stop what?

Paul   Look! It's just a problem with the lights.
It's not as if we're living in one of your
comic books!

Andy   Come on! You're just as freaked out
as I am!

Astro-Man

Narrator   Andy and Paul arguing wakes Dan up. He jumps up.

Dan   What! Who … oh, it's *you* two! What do you want?

Narrator   Dan spots the flashing lights.

Dan   That isn't normal. Hmmm …

Scene 1 Trouble in the toilet

Narrator Dan goes into the hallway to take a look around.

Paul "Ooh I'm Dan, I'm going to fix everything because I'm so clever."

Andy Ha, ha, ha!

Dan Shut up, you two!

Narrator The boys hear a low hum.

Dan What's that sound? It sounds like there's something inside the house.

Narrator Suddenly the lights go off. The hum gets louder. Objects start to shake.

Dan The lights have gone out!

Paul Tell us something we don't know!

Astro-Man

Narrator	The humming sound gets even louder.

Dan What?

Paul I said tell us something we don't …

Narrator	The humming sound is very close.

Paul Eh? What is that?

Andy Whatever is making the weird noise is getting closer.

Dan What?

Narrator	The noise is all around and they all panic.

Dan Argh!

Andy Argh!

Paul Argh!

Scene 1 Trouble in the toilet

Narrator The three boys run and trip over each other. They land next to the door of the downstairs toilet.

Dan Ooof!

Andy Ooof!

Paul Ooof! Ow! I've done something to my arm. My days as a DJ are over!

Andy Oh, really Paul. There are bigger things to worry about at the moment.

Dan Look! There's a light coming from …

Andy Yes. A light coming from the …

Paul Yes. It *is* coming from the toilet!

Astro-Man

Narrator The hallway is lit up by a beam of light. It is coming from behind the toilet door.

Andy I c-c-can hear something.

Dan What?

Andy Something … something moving behind the door.

Narrator The three boys listen.

Paul I really don't like this.

Andy Not so brave now, eh?

Narrator They hear someone clearing his throat.

Dan What was that?

Andy Don't you mean *who*, not what? There's somebody in there!

Dan In the toilet? You mean somebody broke into our toilet?

Scene 1   Trouble in the toilet

Andy   Who breaks into a toilet?

Paul   Well, they must be very brave
or very stupid.

Dan   Huh?

Paul   Well, I wouldn't go in there after you.
At least not for a while!

Narrator   Paul starts banging on the toilet door.

Paul   Hello? Hello? Are you okay in there?
Do you need any help?
How about a gas mask?

Narrator   Paul and Andy are giggling.

Dan   Is this one of your stupid practical
jokes again? It is, isn't it?

Paul   No! But maybe you're the one
playing the joke? Come on, tell us.
What's going on?

Astro-Man

Dan Look I know it's you, come here!

Narrator Dan tries to grab Paul. The boys hear a loud cough from behind the door.

Dan Who's in there?

Narrator The door opens. They see a large boot and a leg with huge muscles.

Dan Oh my …

Paul Help!

Andy But it can't be …

Narrator Dan passes out.

Paul Quick, help Dan up.

Narrator Andy is too shocked to help. Paul shakes Dan awake.

Scene 1   Trouble in the toilet

Andy   It … it looks like …

Paul   What is it? Do you know who he is?

Andy   I, I think I know him, but …

Narrator   They see a large man pull the toilet door off its frame and toss it aside.

Dan   The door! Mum and Dad are not going to be happy when they …

Andy   Doctor M! But, it can't be!

Doctor M   Ha ha ha ha, my plan worked!

Scene 2
DOCTOR M

Narrator The boys are whispering to each other. Doctor M is wearing a green and yellow outfit, with a cape and a mask.

Paul Andy? Isn't that …?

Andy Well, if he wasn't standing in front of us I wouldn't believe it but …

Paul But it's Doctor M isn't it?
Like in your comic.

Doctor M Correct! I am the greatest, the most evil, the most cunning Doctor M!

Astro-Man

Dan He has got to be kidding!

Andy I told you something weird was going on.

Paul Yeah, well, I guess you were right.

Andy But it doesn't make any sense.

Doctor M No? Then perhaps I should explain a few things to you … Andy.

Dan He knows your name!

Paul But, but how …?

Narrator Doctor M turns to Paul and Dan. He bends down and leans in close.

Doctor M Have you two quite finished? Can we carry on?

Paul Erm, sorry.

Dan Yeah, sorry Mister M.

Scene 2   Doctor M

Doctor M   It's *Doctor* M you fool! Now, where
was I? Andy, I expect you would
like to know what is going on?

Andy   This can't be happening!
I made you up in one of my comics.
You're … you're not real.

Doctor M   Oh, but I am young Andy.
And it's all thanks to you.

Andy   Thanks to me? I drew you
in my comics but …

Doctor M   Yes you did. I am Doctor M,
Astro-Man's greatest enemy!

Andy   And now you're here,
in a downstairs toilet?

Dan   With a wet foot!

Paul   Ha ha!

Narrator   Doctor M is angry. He turns to Andy.

Astro-Man

Doctor M Did you really think that *you* invented *me* when you were making your little comic? Did you think that *I*, the great Doctor M, was *your* idea? Ha! I chose to come to you.

Andy What do you mean?

Doctor M Where I am from, people do not eat food. They feed from the imagination of others. From people like you.

Scene 2   Doctor M

Andy   But I don't understand.

Doctor M When you dream Andy,
your imagination creates a world.
That world ends when you wake.
My world is like your dream world.

Dan   Huh? He's not making any sense!

Paul   What's he talking about?

Andy   I don't know.

Doctor M As I was saying. Now I have found you,
Andy, I can begin my plan.

Andy   What plan?

Doctor M I know all about you, Andy.
I know about the comics you draw
and the people you invent.
I started to think … if I can see
Andy's comics in his dreams …
then maybe I could send him
ideas as well.

Astro-Man

Andy   You mean …?

Paul   What does he mean?

Dan   Yeah, what does he mean?

Doctor M I mean Andy, I gave you the idea
to put me in to your comics.
When you drew me for the first time –
it wasn't your idea.

Andy   I don't get it.

Doctor M You were drawing the images
I had sent you.

Andy   But, but why?

Paul   Yeah, why?

Doctor M Why? I was bored. The ideas
I fed upon started to make me wonder
if I was missing out on anything.
So many stories, such adventures!
So I decided to come to your
little world.

Scene 2   Doctor M

Andy   But how did you …?

Dan   Yeah, how did you get here?

Doctor M I came here through your little comic,
             Andy. You left it on the toilet floor.
             So here I am.

Narrator As Doctor M talks, Paul whispers
              to Andy and Dan.

Paul   This can't be happening.
             There's a man in pants and a cape,
             with a wet foot, standing in my toilet
             making no sense at all!

Andy   Shut up Paul, this is serious.

Dan   Yeah, but it's pretty cool too!

Paul I can't wait to tell people at school. We've got a superhero in our house!

Andy This isn't cool. He's not a superhero – he's a baddie.

Dan *So?*

Andy So, he could get us into trouble.

Paul Maybe Andy has a point.

Dan Or maybe you two are just losers.

Narrator Andy turns to Doctor M.

Andy So now you're here, what do you want? Adventure?

Doctor M Why yes! The best kind. Evil adventures … like taking over the world. Ha ha ha ha!

Scene 3

AN EVIL PLAN

Andy So you really are evil then?

Doctor M Yes, and what's best of all, in your world there is no Astro …

Narrator Doctor M suddenly stops mid-sentence.

Andy No who?

Doctor M Nothing, nothing, forget it!

Andy Okay, Doctor M. Well, don't let us get in your way. The door's just over there.

Doctor M   What? No one gets in my way, little boy! Anyway, there is one other thing ...

Andy   Yes?

Doctor M   I need your help.

Paul   Our help?

Dan   What kind of help?

Doctor M   Not help from you two, just Andy!

Andy   How?

Doctor M   Okay, well, you see. Even though I am *here* ... well, I cannot really do anything unless Andy lets me. In a way, he made me.

Dan   Hang on. Don't you have any powers of your own then?

Doctor M   Well, not exactly ...

Dan   Which makes little Andy your master.

Scene 3   An evil plan

Narrator   Doctor M is angry.

Doctor M   I am not a puppet!

Dan   But you can't use your powers unless Andy says so, right?

Doctor M   Well, yes. But I am not …

Dan   A puppet, yeah we know.
So, Andy mate, how about
we take Mister Weird here for a spin?
You know, take him down to school
and get him to turn the head teacher
into a donkey, ha ha!

Astro-Man

Andy What? No, don't be silly.

Dan What's the matter with you? Scared?

Andy No.

Dan Yeah you are. You little baby.

Paul Hmm … I could do with some new decks and some new records too. We could get Doctor M to …

Doctor M Well, I can do those things too. Not exactly what I had in mind, but it's a start. Turn the head teacher into a donkey, ha ha ha ha.

Scene 3 An evil plan

Narrator Paul turns to Andy.

Paul Well?

Andy No! I don't want to get into
any trouble.

Dan What a loser. You're no fun at all.

Paul Think of all the cool things we could do
with Doctor M's powers …

Andy Stop it! All of you, stop it!

Narrator Doctor M holds out his gloved hand
to Andy.

Doctor M Join forces with me, Andy.
Let the terror begin.

Andy This isn't right. I don't want to do
bad things.

Astro-Man

Doctor M   But listen to your friends, Andy.
They want you to help me.
I can give you anything you have
ever dreamed of …

Andy   I need to take it all in.
It's a bit of a shock.

Doctor M   I need an answer by midnight.
Be back here and ready to help me
with my plans or else!

Andy   Or else what?

Doctor M   Or else you and your little friends will
be very sorry. I will hide myself away
until midnight, Andy. But then I will be
waiting for you!

Narrator   Doctor M leaves. Dan and Paul try
to make Andy change his mind.

Paul   Come on Andy, you heard Doctor M.
There will be trouble if we don't help him.

Scene 3   An evil plan

Dan   Yeah. I don't want to miss this
             chance, so you had better change
             your mind quick.

Andy   But it's not right. Doctor M is evil.

Dan   I don't care about that. He said we
             could have anything we like. *Anything!*
             Just think what we could do.

Paul   Maybe we could help him just a little
             bit? You know, have a laugh and then
             send him home.

Andy   *How?* How could we
             send him home?
             He's evil and he's got
             super powers.
             It's just too dangerous.

Scene 4

ANDY THINKS FAST

Narrator	Andy, Paul and Dan are still talking about Doctor M.

Paul   So, what are we going to do?

Andy   I think I need to look at my comics.

Dan   Do you really think this is the time for reading your stupid comics?

Andy   Yes, I do. Doctor M came out of one of my comics remember!

Paul   Yeah, maybe Andy's right.

Astro-Man

Andy   Let's all go to my house.

Dan   Okay, but remember, I still want to turn the head teacher into a donkey.

Narrator   Andy, Paul and Dan race to Andy's home. Andy looks through his comics and drawings for an answer.

Andy   Think! Think!

Dan   This is such a waste of time.

Paul   Shut up, Dan! Andy's the one who knows all about comics.

Andy   Will you two just stop it?
I need to think …
I need a plan to get rid
of Doctor M.

Dan   Well, if you're not going to help Doctor M, then I'm off.

Andy   Good!

Scene 4   Andy thinks fast

Dan   You started this mess by drawing Doctor M, so you can be the one to sort it out!

Andy and **Paul** (*together*)
Fine!

Narrator   Dan leaves. Andy finds a picture of a superhero he invented – Astro-Man.

Andy   Yes, that's it! I think Doctor M has made a very big mistake.

Paul   What do you mean?

Andy   Well, do you remember he said something about Astro-Man? That he was glad Astro-Man wasn't here on Earth.

Paul   Hang on, oh yeah, what was it he said? "In your world there is no …"

Andy   "There is no Astro-Man."

Paul   Which means?

Andy	Which means there's probably an Astro-Man where Doctor M comes from!
Paul	I don't get it.
Andy	Don't you see? If Doctor M can put his image into my head so I draw him … maybe I could try to contact Astro-Man?
Paul	I still don't get it.
Andy	Okay. I'll draw a new comic story. In it I'll ask Astro-Man to come and save us from Doctor M. Then maybe it will work and Astro-Man will come!
Paul	My head really hurts!
Narrator	It is close to midnight. Paul and Andy are waiting by the downstairs toilet. Suddenly, Doctor M appears.

Scene 4   Andy thinks fast

Doctor M   Well, I expect you have decided
to help me?

Andy   Yes. I have.

Narrator   Andy reaches for a comic book
in his back pocket and opens it up.
He lays it on the ground in front
of Doctor M.

Doctor M   What is this?
More of your childish drawings!
Don't ask me to make you
better at drawing.
I'm not sure even my powers
could stretch to that.
Ha ha ha ha!

Astro-Man

Paul If anyone spoke about my DJ skills
like that I'd …

Doctor M You would do what?

Andy We … would … do … this … NOW!

Narrator Suddenly a lightning bolt flies
from the pages of the comic book.
It takes on a shape as it grows
bigger and bigger.

Doctor M What trickery is this?

Narrator The shape becomes Astro-Man.

Doctor M Nooo! Astro-Man!

Astro-Man Did you think you could escape me,
Doctor M? Things have been very quiet
without you around, so I began
looking for you. I never thought
I'd find you in a toilet!

Scene 4   Andy thinks fast

Doctor M   But, but how *did* you find me?

Astro-Man If it wasn't for this brave young man,
I wouldn't have.

Doctor M   You heroes are always
spoiling my fun.

Astro-Man Andy is the real hero.

Narrator   Astro-Man lifts Doctor M off the ground
and dangles him by his cape.

Doctor M   You're such a show off!

Astro-Man We're going back home now,
Prisoner M. I have an
astro-prison cell waiting for you.

Doctor M   Oh yes, very good
you astro-idiot!

Astro-Man

Narrator Astro-Man turns to Andy and Paul.

Astro-Man Thank you for your help.
It can't have been easy to refuse
Doctor M. I'm sure he tempted you
with promises of great things.
I'm glad to see you are both honest.

Narrator Paul's face turns red.
He feels uncomfortable.

Andy Astro-Man, I still don't really
understand. Did I invent you?
Or did you *make* me invent you?

Astro-Man Andy, having an imagination
is one of the most important things
anyone can have. It doesn't matter
where the ideas come from, just as
long as you have them. You are
a talented young man and an
honest one. You should feel proud.

Scene 4 Andy thinks fast

Narrator Andy's face begins to glow with pride.

Paul And what about me? If Andy is a hero, then … well … does that make me a sidekick?

Narrator As the figures of Astro-Man and Doctor M fade, Astro-Man looks back and smiles at Paul.

Astro-Man Paul, you are much more than a sidekick. You are a true hero … and a wicked DJ!

In the chatroom...

Pretend you are Astro-Man! On the 'Supernet' (the Internet for superheroes), you see this message:

Chat Room | Ringtones | Music | Movies | Advice

Message posted by Power Boy

All my friends want me to use my powers to get them stuff. I don't usually mind helping my mates, but I don't want to do bad things.

How do I stand up to them, but still keep them as friends?

- Write an email from Astro-Man to Power Boy, giving him some ideas of how he could say 'No' to his friends.

Astro-Man

ROLE PLAY...

Work in a group of three. Take the parts of Doctor M, Astro-Man and Andy. Andy is in the middle of Astro-Man and Doctor M. They have to try and get him to take their side.

- What would Doctor M say to Andy to make him help him do evil things?
- What would Astro-Man say to Andy to keep him on the side of the goodies?
- Andy must decide who to join with.

IN PAIRS...

- *Work with a partner. Look back through the play and note down the words that describe Doctor M. Look for words that describe what he looks like, and words that describe his personality.*
- *Draw a picture of Doctor M and label it with the words you picked out.*

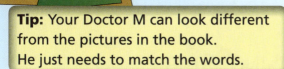

Tip: Your Doctor M can look different from the pictures in the book.
He just needs to match the words.

47

Astro-Man
Buried Alive
Dumped!
Foul Play
Plane Crazy
Step Wars
Toffee Nose
Yard

Interact plays are available from booksellers or
www.risingstars-uk.com

For more information please call 0871 47 23 010